NETWORK MARKETING SIMPLIFIED

"Unveiling the Power of Network Marketing: A Simplified Guide to Success"

VINCENT SIMS

Copyright © 2023
All rights reserved by Vincent Sims

Moral Rights

Vincent Sims asserts the moral right to be identified as the author of this work.

External Content

Vincent Sims has no responsibility for the persistence or accuracy of URLs for external or third-party Internet Websites referred to in this publication and does not guarantee that any content on such Websites is, or will remain, accurate or appropriate.

Dedication

"To all aspiring entrepreneurs navigating the intricate web of possibilities, this book is dedicated to simplifying the essence of network marketing. May these pages empower you with clarity, insights, and a roadmap for success in the dynamic world of network marketing. Here's to your journey of simplifying the complexities and unlocking the true potential of your network."

Table of Contents

Acknowledgments

"I extend my heartfelt gratitude to those who have contributed to the creation of this book, 'Network Marketing Simplified.' Special thanks to my mentors and industry leaders whose wisdom has illuminated the path. To the tireless network marketers whose stories enrich these pages, thank you for sharing your experiences. My appreciation also goes to friends, family, and readers – your support has been invaluable. This work is a collective effort, and I am grateful for each person who played a role in simplifying the intricate world of network marketing."

Preface

"In embarking on the journey of 'Network Marketing Simplified,' I recognized the need for a compass in the often labyrinthine landscape of network marketing. This book aims to be that guide—a distillation of insights, strategies, and practical wisdom that demystifies the intricacies of network marketing.

As we delve into these pages, I intend to empower you with a clearer understanding of the principles that underpin successful network marketing endeavors. Drawing from real-world experiences, industry best practices, and a commitment to simplicity, this book serves as a roadmap for both beginners and seasoned entrepreneurs.

Network marketing, at its core, is about connections—connections that transcend products and profits. It's about building relationships, fostering trust, and creating a network that propels you toward your goals. 'Network Marketing Simplified' is not just a guide; it's a tool to help you navigate this dynamic landscape with confidence and purpose.

I invite you to embark on this journey with an open mind and a readiness to simplify the complexities. May this book be a valuable companion in your pursuit of success and fulfillment in the world of network marketing."

Foreword

"In an era of interconnected possibilities, 'Network Marketing Simplified' emerges as a beacon of clarity in a realm often clouded by misconceptions. As we navigate the dynamic landscape of network marketing, this book stands as a testament to the power of simplification.

As someone who has witnessed the transformative potential of network marketing, I am delighted to introduce this guide—a resource designed to demystify the intricacies and empower individuals to harness the true essence of this industry.

The author's dedication to clarity, coupled with a wealth of experience, resonates throughout these pages. From fundamental principles to nuanced strategies, 'Network Marketing Simplified' offers a comprehensive toolkit for both novices and seasoned professionals alike.

This book transcends the conventional narratives surrounding network marketing, emphasizing the importance of genuine connections, ethical practices, and a holistic approach to business. It is not merely a guide; it is an invitation to rethink and redefine success in the context of network marketing.

As you embark on this journey, may 'Network Marketing Simplified' be your trusted companion, providing insights, inspiration, and actionable steps to navigate the exciting and often misunderstood world of network marketing. Here's to your simplified path to success."

Chapter 1:

Introduction to Network Marketing

- Understanding the Basics

Network marketing, often referred to as multi-level marketing (MLM), is a business model that relies on a network of distributors or representatives to sell products or services. The essence of this model lies in building a network of individuals who not only sell but also recruit others into the network, creating a hierarchical structure.

1. Building Relationships:

At the core of network marketing is the emphasis on building relationships. Successful network marketers understand the value of personal connections and word-of-mouth marketing. The trust established within a network often leads to more effective sales and sustainable business growth.

2. Hierarchical Structure:

Network marketing operates on a hierarchical structure where each distributor has the opportunity to build their team. As a distributor recruits others, they become part of the recruiter's downline. Commissions and bonuses are often based on the sales generated by one's downline, creating a structure that encourages teamwork and mentorship.

3. Compensation Plans:

One distinctive feature of network marketing is its various compensation plans. These plans outline how distributors are compensated for their sales and the sales of their downline. Common compensation structures include binary, matrix, and unilevel plans, each with its own set of rules and benefits.

4. Product Knowledge and Passion:

Successful network marketers are not just salespeople; they are passionate advocates for the products or services they represent. In-depth knowledge about the offerings enables distributors to effectively communicate the value to potential customers and recruits.

5. Training and Support:

A robust support system is crucial in network marketing. Reputable companies provide training sessions, marketing materials, and ongoing support to help distributors succeed. This collaborative environment fosters a sense of community and ensures that everyone has the tools they need to thrive.

6. Ethical Practices:

Maintaining integrity is key to the long-term success of network marketing. Ethical practices involve transparent communication, honesty about potential earnings, and a focus on delivering value to customers. Unethical practices can tarnish reputations and undermine the trust within the network.

7. Persistence and Resilience:

Network marketing is not a get-rich-quick scheme. Success often requires persistence, resilience, and a long-term perspective. Building a network takes time, and individuals who stay committed to the process are more likely to reap the rewards over time.

Understanding these basics provides a foundation for navigating the world of network marketing. Whether you're considering joining a network marketing opportunity or already involved, focusing on building genuine relationships, mastering product knowledge, and embracing ethical practices can contribute to a fulfilling and successful journey in this dynamic industry.

- Historical Perspective

Network marketing, also known as multi-level marketing (MLM), has a historical perspective rooted in the mid-20th century. Its origins can be traced back to companies like Nutrilite, which was founded in the 1930s by Carl Rehnborg. Nutrilite utilized a direct selling model that involved distributors building networks to sell products.

However, it was in the 1940s that the modern concept of network marketing began to take shape with the establishment of the California Vitamin Company, later known as Nutrilite. This company introduced the idea of compensating distributors not only for their sales but also for the sales made by the distributors they recruited – creating a multi-level commission structure.

In the 1950s, the Amway Corporation emerged as a prominent player in the network marketing industry. Founded by Jay Van Andel and Richard DeVos, Amway adopted the multi-level marketing model and became a pioneer in developing a comprehensive network marketing system. The success of Amway played a significant role in popularizing the concept of building a sales force through a network of independent distributors.

Throughout the latter half of the 20th century, network marketing faced both acclaim and criticism. Advocates praised its potential for entrepreneurial success and the opportunity it provided to individuals to build their businesses with minimal capital. However, detractors raised concerns about the pyramid-like structure of some MLM companies and the potential for exploitation.

The 21st century witnessed the continued evolution of network marketing with the rise of numerous companies utilizing MLM structures. The industry expanded globally, offering a diverse range of products and services through direct selling and network building. The advent of the internet and social media further transformed the landscape, providing new avenues for distributors to connect with potential customers and recruit team members.

Despite its enduring presence, network marketing has faced regulatory scrutiny in various countries, with legal and ethical considerations shaping the industry's practices. While some view it as a legitimate business model empowering individuals, others remain skeptical, emphasizing the importance of due diligence and transparency in MLM ventures.

In summary, the historical perspective of network marketing reveals a journey from its early roots in the mid-20th century to becoming a global industry with both fervent supporters and vocal critics. The ongoing evolution of the sector reflects its adaptability to changing times and technologies, shaping the way network marketing is perceived and practiced today.

- Key Concepts and Terminology

Network marketing involves a unique set of concepts and terminology essential for understanding its structure and operations. Here are key terms associated with network marketing:

1. Upline and Downline:

- Upline: Refers to the distributors who are positioned higher in the network hierarchy and are responsible for recruiting and supporting those below them.

- Downline: Encompasses the distributors recruited by an individual, forming a hierarchical structure of team members.

2. Compensation Plan:

- The framework outlining how distributors are compensated for their sales and the sales generated by their downline. Common structures include binary, matrix, and unilevel plans.

3. PV (Personal Volume) and GV (Group Volume):

- PV: The sales volume generated by a distributor's personal sales.

- GV: The cumulative sales volume within a distributor's entire downline organization.

4. Sponsorship:

- The process of recruiting new distributors into the network. Sponsors guide and support their recruits, earning bonuses based on the recruits' sales.

5. MLM (Multi-Level Marketing):

- A business model where salespersons earn income through direct sales of products/services and by recruiting a team of distributors. Commissions are earned on both personal sales and the sales of the downline.

6. Duplication:

- The practice of replicating successful strategies and actions within a network. Successful duplication leads to the growth and sustainability of the network.

7. Binary System:

- A compensation plan where distributors build two legs (teams) under them. Commissions are often based on the sales volume of the weaker leg, encouraging balanced growth.

8. Matrix System:

- Distributors are limited in the number of recruits they can sponsor on their first level. This structure fosters teamwork and spill-over effects.

9. Unilevel System:

- A compensation plan where distributors can sponsor unlimited recruits on their frontline. Commissions are earned based on sales volume throughout the entire downline.

10. Autoship:

- A system requiring distributors to make regular purchases of products to remain eligible for commissions. This ensures ongoing product movement within the network.

11. Rank Advancement:

- The progression of distributors through various leadership levels based on their sales volume, recruitment, and team building achievements. Higher ranks often come with increased bonuses and incentives.

12. Breakaway:

- A point in a distributor's career where they "break away" from their upline, becoming an independent leader with their organization. This often triggers increased commissions and responsibilities.

Understanding these key concepts and terminology is crucial for individuals involved in network marketing, enabling them to navigate the intricacies of the business model, set realistic goals, and effectively manage their teams for success.

Chapter 2:

The Power of Relationships in Network Marketing

- Building Strong Connections

Building strong connections in network marketing is crucial for long-term success. Start by genuinely getting to know your team members and understanding their goals, strengths, and challenges. Regular communication is key; foster an environment where everyone feels heard and valued.

Provide support and guidance to your team members. Help them develop their skills and overcome obstacles. A strong mentorship can create a sense of trust and loyalty, enhancing the overall network.

Encourage collaboration among team members. Facilitate team meetings, where ideas can be shared, and strategies can be discussed. A collaborative environment fosters a sense of unity and shared purpose, strengthening the bond within the network.

Recognition is a powerful tool in network marketing. Acknowledge and celebrate achievements, both big and small. This not only motivates individuals but also reinforces the sense of belonging and accomplishment.

Maintain transparency in your communication. Be honest about challenges and changes within the network. Transparency builds trust, and trust is the foundation of any strong relationship.

Incorporate team-building activities and events. These not only provide an opportunity for socializing but also help in creating a positive and cohesive team culture.

Invest time in continuous education and training. When team members feel that their professional development is a priority, they are more likely to stay engaged and committed.

Lastly, lead by example. Demonstrate the values and work ethic you expect from your team. A leader who embodies the principles of hard work, integrity, and dedication will inspire others to follow suit, creating a network marked by strong connections and mutual success.

- Trust and Credibility

Trust and credibility play pivotal roles in the realm of network marketing. Building and maintaining trust is essential for the success of any network marketing venture. Here are key aspects to consider:

1. Transparency:
  - Be transparent about your products or services. Clearly communicate what you offer, how it works, and any associated costs. Transparency fosters trust and helps build a credible reputation.

2. Consistent Communication:
  - Regular and consistent communication is vital. Keep your network informed about updates, promotions, and any changes. This helps in creating a reliable and trustworthy image.

3. Customer Testimonials:

- Positive experiences from satisfied customers can be powerful tools for building trust. Encourage customers to share their testimonials and success stories. Authenticity is key here.

4. Professionalism:

- Present yourself and your business in a professional manner. This includes your online presence, communication style, and overall conduct. Professionalism instills confidence in your network.

5. Compliance and Ethics:

- Adhere to legal and ethical standards. Make sure your network marketing practices comply with industry regulations. Unethical practices can quickly erode trust and credibility.

6. Training and Support:

- Provide adequate training and support to your network members. When they feel equipped and supported, they are more likely to trust the business model and you as a leader.

7. Consistent Results:

- Consistency in delivering promised results is crucial. Whether it's product quality, service delivery, or income potential, consistency builds trust over time.

8. Long-Term Vision:

- Emphasize a long-term vision for your network marketing business. This not only builds confidence in the stability of your venture but also reinforces the idea that you are committed to mutual success.

9. Responsive Customer Service:

- A prompt and helpful customer service system contributes significantly to trust. Address concerns and inquiries promptly, showing that you value your customers' opinions.

10. Educational Content:

- Share educational content about your products, industry trends, and successful strategies. This positions you as an authority in your field and enhances your credibility.

In network marketing, trust and credibility are the foundation of lasting relationships. By prioritizing these elements, you create an environment where your network feels secure, motivated, and more likely to contribute to the overall success of the business.

- Leveraging Personal and Professional Networks

Building and leveraging personal and professional networks is a crucial aspect of personal and career development. Your network can open doors to new opportunities, provide valuable insights, and offer support during both personal and professional challenges.

1. Building Strong Foundations:

   - Invest time in cultivating genuine connections. Attend industry events, conferences, and social gatherings to meet like-minded individuals.

   - Utilize online platforms such as LinkedIn to connect with professionals in your field. Personalize connection requests to make a lasting impression.

2. Reciprocity and Support:

- Networks thrive on reciprocity. Offer assistance when possible and be willing to share your knowledge and resources.

- Building a support system within your network ensures that you have people to turn to for advice or collaboration.

3. Information Exchange:

- Stay informed about industry trends and news. Your network can be a valuable source of information, providing insights that might not be readily available through other channels.

- Regularly share relevant content and updates with your network to position yourself as a valuable resource.

4. Professional Development:

- Seek mentorship within your network. Experienced individuals can provide guidance and share their experiences, helping you navigate your career path more effectively.

- Join professional groups and forums related to your field. Engaging in discussions can broaden your perspectives and expose you to diverse ideas.

5. Job Opportunities:

- Leverage your network when exploring new job opportunities. Many positions are filled through referrals, and having a strong network increases your chances of being connected to potential employers.

- Keep your network updated on your skills and achievements, making it easier for them to recommend you when opportunities arise.

6. Diversification of Contacts:

- Aim for a diverse network. Connecting with individuals from different industries and backgrounds can bring fresh perspectives and ideas.

- Attend networking events beyond your immediate professional circle to broaden your reach and increase the diversity of your connections.

7. Nurture Relationships:

 - Regularly check in with your network. A simple message or occasional catch-up can strengthen your connections and keep you top-of-mind.

 - Celebrate the successes of your network members and offer support during challenging times. Genuine relationships go beyond professional interests.

8. Soft Skills Enhancement:

 - Networking enhances your interpersonal skills. Practice active listening, effective communication, and empathy, as these skills are invaluable in building lasting connections.

By proactively building and leveraging your personal and professional networks, you not only enhance your career prospects but also contribute to a mutually beneficial community where knowledge and opportunities flow freely.

Chapter 3:

Choosing the Right Network Marketing Company

- Researching Opportunities

Selecting the right network marketing company is a critical decision that can significantly impact your success in the industry. Thoroughly researching opportunities ensures that you align with a company that suits your goals and values. Here are essential steps to guide your research:

1. Company Reputation:

   - Investigate the reputation of the network marketing company. Look for reviews, testimonials, and any available feedback from current or past distributors.

- Assess the company's track record, including its history, financial stability, and any legal or ethical issues it may have faced.

2. Product or Service Quality:

- Evaluate the quality and uniqueness of the products or services offered. A company with a strong, marketable product is more likely to attract customers and retain distributors.

- Consider whether the products align with your personal values and interests, as passion for the offerings can enhance your marketing efforts.

3. Compensation Plan:

- Understand the compensation plan in detail. Different companies have varying structures, and it's crucial to choose one that aligns with your financial goals and preferences.

- Look for transparent and fair compensation structures, avoiding companies with complex or unclear payout mechanisms.

4. Training and Support:

- Assess the level of training and support provided by the company. A robust training program can contribute to your success and help you develop the necessary skills.

- Consider the accessibility of support resources, such as mentorship programs, webinars, and educational materials.

5. Company Values and Culture:

- Align yourself with a company whose values resonate with yours. Understanding the corporate culture can influence your overall satisfaction and success in the network marketing venture.

- Evaluate the company's mission, vision, and commitment to ethical business practices.

6. Start-Up Costs and Hidden Fees:

- Be wary of excessive start-up costs or hidden fees. A reputable network marketing company should provide transparency regarding any financial commitments required to join and maintain your distributorship.

- Compare start-up costs with industry standards and assess whether the initial investment is reasonable.

7. Market Trends and Timing:

- Research market trends and assess the timing of joining a particular company. Timing can play a significant role in your success, especially if the products or services are in high demand.

- Consider the growth potential of the company and whether it operates in a sustainable and expanding market.

8. Legal Compliance:

- Ensure that the network marketing company complies with legal regulations and industry standards. Verify its legitimacy by checking its registration, licenses, and adherence to local and international laws.

9. Success Stories:

- Seek out success stories within the company. Hearing about the achievements of other distributors can provide insights into the potential for success and the company's ability to support its members.

10. Gut Feeling:

- Trust your instincts. If something feels off or too good to be true, it's essential to take a step back and reassess the opportunity.

By conducting thorough research and due diligence, you can make an informed decision when choosing a network marketing company, increasing your chances of long-term success in the industry.

- Evaluating Compensation Plans

Evaluating compensation plans is a critical aspect of navigating the landscape of network marketing opportunities. A well-structured compensation plan can significantly impact your success and income potential. Here's a guide on what to consider:

1. Understanding the Basics:

   - Start by understanding the fundamental components of the compensation plan. This includes direct commissions, bonuses, and any additional incentives offered by the company.

2. Commission Structure:

   - Analyze the commission structure to ensure it aligns with your financial goals. Look for plans that offer competitive commissions on both personal sales and team performance.

3. Residual Income:

- Evaluate the sustainability of residual income. A strong compensation plan should provide a reliable stream of income over time, especially from repeat purchases or subscription-based products.

4. Rank Advancements and Bonuses:

- Examine the criteria for rank advancements and associated bonuses. A good plan should reward both personal sales achievements and the growth and success of your team.

5. Qualification Requirements:

- Understand any qualifications or quotas necessary to be eligible for commissions. Be wary of plans that set unrealistic targets or force you to maintain a high level of personal sales to qualify for team bonuses.

6. Product or Service Quality:

- Assess the quality and market demand for the products or services offered. A compensation plan may look attractive, but it's crucial that the underlying products are valuable and meet customer needs.

7. Payout Frequency:

- Consider the frequency of payouts. Some compensation plans offer weekly payouts, while others may have longer payout cycles. Choose a plan that aligns with your financial preferences and needs.

8. Training and Support:

- Evaluate the level of training and support provided by the company. A compensation plan is only as good as the resources available to help you and your team succeed.

9. Company Reputation:

- Research the reputation of the company in the industry. A company with a solid track record is more likely to have a fair and reliable compensation plan. Look for reviews and testimonials from current or former distributors.

10. Long-Term Viability:

- Consider the long-term viability of the compensation plan. Look for plans that promote stability and sustainability rather than those that rely on rapid recruitment without substantial product or service value.

11. Hidden Costs:

- Be aware of any hidden costs or requirements. Some compensation plans may have hidden fees or mandatory purchases that can impact your overall profitability.

By carefully evaluating these aspects of a compensation plan, you can make an informed decision about whether a network marketing opportunity is a good fit for your financial goals and aligns with your values.

- Assessing Product or Service Quality

Assessing the quality of products or services in a network marketing venture is crucial for long-term success and customer satisfaction. Here's a comprehensive guide on how to evaluate the quality of what you are offering:

1. Understand the Product or Service:
   - Begin by gaining a thorough understanding of the product or service. Know its features, benefits, and how it stands out in the market.

2. Customer Feedback:

- Consider customer feedback and reviews. Honest testimonials from actual users provide valuable insights into the real-world performance and satisfaction levels associated with the product or service.

3. Third-Party Certifications:

- Look for any third-party certifications or endorsements. These can validate the quality and safety of the product, adding credibility to your marketing efforts.

4. Ingredients and Components:

- If applicable, scrutinize the ingredients or components of the product. Transparency in this regard builds trust and allows you to communicate effectively with potential customers.

5. Comparative Analysis:

- Compare the product or service with similar offerings in the market. Assess how it measures up in terms of features, price, and overall value. Highlight any unique selling points.

6. Durability and Longevity:

- Evaluate the durability and longevity of the product. A quality product should be built to last, ensuring customer satisfaction and minimizing returns or dissatisfaction.

7. Scientific Basis (if applicable):

- For products making scientific or health-related claims, examine the scientific basis behind these assertions. Ensure that any claims are supported by credible research or studies.

8. Company Reputation:

- Consider the reputation of the company itself. A company with a history of providing high-quality products is more likely to continue delivering excellence.

9. Return Policy:

- Review the company's return policy. A fair and customer-friendly return policy demonstrates confidence in the product's quality and can enhance trust among potential buyers.

10. Customer Support:

- Assess the level of customer support provided by the company. A commitment to excellent customer service indicates a dedication to customer satisfaction and product quality.

11. Product Testing and Quality Control:

- Inquire about the company's product testing and quality control processes. A company that invests in rigorous testing demonstrates a commitment to delivering a reliable and high-quality product.

12. Innovation and Updates:

- Evaluate whether the company demonstrates a commitment to innovation and regularly updates its products. This can indicate responsiveness to market demands and a dedication to improvement.

By carefully assessing the quality of the products or services you are promoting, you not only build trust with your customers but also establish a foundation for long-term success in network marketing. It's the quality of your offerings that ultimately sustains your business and contributes to a positive reputation within the industry.

Chapter 4:

Strategies for Successful Network Marketing

- Effective Communication

Effective communication is a cornerstone of successful network marketing. Clear and compelling communication fosters trust, builds relationships, and drives the growth of your network. Here are key strategies to enhance communication in network marketing:

1. Active Listening:

- Practice active listening to truly understand the needs and concerns of your team members and potential customers. By showing genuine interest, you create a foundation for effective communication.

2. Clear Messaging:

- Craft clear and concise messages about your products, services, and the network marketing opportunity. Avoid jargon and communicate in a way that is easily understood by a diverse audience.

3. Storytelling:

- Utilize storytelling to convey the benefits and success stories associated with your products or business. People connect with narratives, and this can make your message more memorable and relatable.

4. Utilize Various Communication Channels:

- Leverage a variety of communication channels, including social media, email, webinars, and in-person meetings. Different people prefer different mediums, so diversifying your approach ensures broader reach.

5. Provide Value in Content:
 - Share valuable content that educates and informs your audience. Whether it's through blog posts, videos, or social media updates, delivering content that adds value positions you as an authority in your niche.

6. Empower and Motivate:
 - Motivate your team by empowering them with the information and tools they need for success. Regularly communicate goals, recognize achievements, and provide ongoing support to maintain motivation.

7. Consistency in Communication:
 - Establish a consistent communication schedule. Regular updates and check-ins with your team

create a sense of continuity and reliability, fostering a stronger connection.

8. Adapt to Your Audience:
  - Understand the preferences and communication styles of your audience. Whether they prefer formal presentations or casual conversations, adapting your approach enhances receptivity.

9. Address Concerns Promptly:
  - Actively address concerns and inquiries promptly. This demonstrates a commitment to customer service and reinforces trust within your network.

10. Training and Development Programs:
  - Implement effective training programs that provide your team with the knowledge and skills they need. Clear communication about training schedules and resources contributes to team development.

11. Encourage Two-Way Communication:

    - Foster an environment where open communication is encouraged. This includes welcoming feedback, ideas, and concerns from your team members. Two-way communication builds a sense of collaboration and mutual respect.

12. Use Positive Language:

    - Choose positive and empowering language in your communication. Positive messaging not only motivates but also creates an optimistic and uplifting atmosphere within your network.

By prioritizing effective communication in your network marketing efforts, you create a solid foundation for building and sustaining a successful team. Clear, honest, and engaging communication fosters a positive network culture, where everyone feels valued and motivated to contribute to the collective success.

- Goal Setting and Planning

Goal setting and planning are essential components of success in any endeavor, including network marketing. By establishing clear objectives and developing a strategic plan, you can chart a course toward achievement and long-term prosperity. Here's a guide to effective goal setting and planning in the context of network marketing:

1. Define Clear and Specific Goals:
   - Begin by clearly defining your goals. Make them specific, measurable, achievable, relevant, and time-bound (SMART). Whether it's a sales target, team expansion, or rank advancement, specificity provides clarity.

2. Prioritize Your Goals:

- Prioritize your goals based on their importance and impact. This helps in allocating resources and efforts efficiently, ensuring that you focus on the most critical aspects of your network marketing business.

3. Break Down Goals into Milestones:

- Break down larger goals into smaller, manageable milestones. Achieving these milestones provides a sense of accomplishment and keeps motivation high as you work towards the bigger objectives.

4. Create an Action Plan:

- Develop a detailed action plan outlining the steps required to reach each goal. This plan should include specific tasks, deadlines, and the resources needed for successful execution.

5. Set Realistic Timeframes:

- Be realistic about the time required to achieve your goals. Setting overly ambitious timelines can lead to frustration, while realistic deadlines promote steady progress and maintain motivation.

6. Regularly Review and Adjust:

- Regularly review your goals and progress. Network marketing is dynamic, and adjustments may be necessary. Assess what is working, what needs improvement, and adapt your plan accordingly.

7. Focus on Activities, Not Just Outcomes:

- While outcomes are important, focus on the daily activities that contribute to your goals. Consistent, high-quality efforts in areas such as prospecting, follow-ups, and team support ultimately lead to success.

8. Visualize Success:

- Use visualization techniques to imagine the successful realization of your goals. Visualization can enhance motivation and create a positive mindset, crucial for overcoming challenges.

9. Accountability Partner:

- Share your goals with a trusted friend, mentor, or teammate who can act as an accountability partner. Regular check-ins and discussions about progress can provide valuable insights and motivation.

10. Celebrate Achievements:

- Celebrate both small and significant achievements. Acknowledging milestones boosts morale and reinforces the positive aspects of your network marketing journey.

11. Continuous Learning and Adaptation:

- Embrace a mindset of continuous learning. Stay informed about industry trends, effective marketing strategies, and leadership skills. The ability to adapt and evolve is key to long-term success.

12. Balance Short-Term and Long-Term Goals:

- Strike a balance between short-term and long-term goals. While immediate wins are gratifying, it's crucial to align them with the broader vision and direction of your network marketing business.

By integrating goal setting and planning into your network marketing approach, you create a roadmap for success. These practices not only provide direction but also instill discipline, motivation, and resilience – essential qualities for navigating the dynamic landscape of network marketing.

- **Leveraging Social Media**

Leveraging social media is a powerful strategy in the realm of network marketing, providing a dynamic platform to connect with a vast audience, build relationships, and promote products or services. Here's a comprehensive guide on effectively using social media for network marketing success:

1. Choose the Right Platforms:
   - Identify the social media platforms that align with your target audience and business goals. Platforms like Facebook, Instagram, LinkedIn, and Twitter offer diverse opportunities for network marketing.

2. Optimize Profiles:
   - Ensure your social media profiles are optimized for professionalism and reflect your brand identity.

Use high-quality visuals, a compelling bio, and relevant links to create a positive first impression.

3. Content Strategy:

- Develop a content strategy that blends promotional content with valuable, shareable, and engaging information. This could include product highlights, success stories, educational content, and behind-the-scenes glimpses.

4. Consistent Branding:

- Maintain consistent branding across all your social media channels. Consistency in visuals, messaging, and tone reinforces your brand identity and builds brand recognition.

5. Engage with Your Audience:

- Actively engage with your audience by responding to comments, messages, and participating in relevant discussions. Engagement fosters a sense of community and trust.

6. Utilize Visual Content:

- Visual content, such as images and videos, tends to perform well on social media. Use visually appealing content to showcase your products, share testimonials, and tell your network marketing story.

7. Leverage Hashtags:

- Research and use relevant hashtags to expand the reach of your posts. Hashtags help your content get discovered by individuals interested in topics related to your products or industry.

8. Host Live Events:

- Take advantage of live features on platforms like Facebook and Instagram. Host live Q&A sessions, product demonstrations, or behind-the-scenes glimpses to engage your audience in real-time.

9. Run Contests and Giveaways:

- Running contests or giveaways can generate excitement and increase your social media reach. Encourage participants to share your content to amplify its impact.

10. Network with Influencers:

- Identify and connect with influencers in your industry. Collaborating with influencers can extend your reach and lend credibility to your network marketing efforts.

11. Paid Advertising:

- Consider investing in paid advertising to target specific demographics and increase visibility. Platforms like Facebook and Instagram offer targeted advertising options for network marketers.

12. Analytics and Optimization:

- Regularly analyze the performance of your social media efforts using analytics tools provided by each platform. Use these insights to refine your strategy, focusing on what works best for your audience.

13. Educate and Add Value:

- Position yourself as an expert in your field by sharing educational content. Offer tips, insights, and valuable information related to your products or services, establishing trust and credibility.

14. Build Relationships, Not Just Sales:

- Network marketing is about relationships. Focus on building authentic connections rather than solely pushing for sales. Genuine interactions lead to a loyal and engaged network.

By strategically leveraging social media, you can amplify your network marketing efforts, reach a broader audience, and create a vibrant online community. Consistency, authenticity, and a focus on value-driven content are key to building a successful presence on social media platforms.

Chapter 5:

Overcoming Challenges in Network Marketing

- Handling Rejections

Handling rejections is an inevitable aspect of network marketing, and mastering this challenge is crucial for long-term success. Here's a guide on overcoming rejection and using it as a stepping stone in your network marketing journey:

1. Develop a Resilient Mindset:
   - Understand that rejection is a natural part of any sales-oriented business, including network marketing. Cultivate a resilient mindset that sees rejection as an opportunity for growth rather than a setback.

2. Separate the Person from the Product:

- Encourage your team and yourself to separate personal worth from the rejection of your product or opportunity. Rejections are often about timing, preferences, or circumstances rather than a reflection of your value.

3. Learn from Rejections:

- Treat each rejection as a learning experience. Ask for feedback if appropriate, and use the insights to refine your approach. Continuous improvement is key to overcoming challenges in network marketing.

4. Focus on the Positive Interactions:

- Shift your focus from rejections to positive interactions. Celebrate every successful sale, recruit, or positive feedback. Redirecting your attention to the positive aspects of your journey helps maintain motivation.

5. Understand the "No" Isn't Personal:

- Recognize that when someone says "no," it's not a rejection of you as an individual. It may be a "no" to the opportunity at that moment, and it doesn't diminish your value or potential for success.

6. Refine Your Approach:

- Use rejections as an opportunity to refine your approach. Analyze common objections and develop strategies to address them proactively. Continuous refinement of your pitch enhances your effectiveness over time.

7. Build a Support System:

- Surround yourself with a supportive network, both within your team and outside of it. Share experiences, seek advice, and draw encouragement from those who understand the challenges of network marketing.

8. Reframe Rejections as Temporary Setbacks:

- View rejections as temporary setbacks rather than permanent failures. Adopting a growth mindset allows you to see challenges as opportunities for learning and improvement.

9. Maintain a Positive Attitude:

- Cultivate a positive attitude that persists even in the face of rejection. Positivity is contagious and can influence your interactions, making them more appealing to potential customers or team members.

10. Set Realistic Expectations:

- Understand that not everyone will be interested or ready to join your network at the moment you approach them. Setting realistic expectations helps in managing disappointment and staying focused on long-term success.

11. Celebrate Your Efforts:

- Acknowledge and celebrate your efforts, regardless of the outcome. The fact that you are actively engaging in network marketing, facing challenges, and learning from experiences is an achievement in itself.

12. Focus on Building Relationships:
- Shift your focus from immediate results to building genuine relationships. By prioritizing relationships over transactions, you create a foundation for sustained success, even if the initial interaction results in a rejection.

Handling rejections in network marketing is a skill that improves with practice and a positive mindset. By embracing rejection as a natural part of the journey and leveraging it as an opportunity for growth, you position yourself for long-term success in the dynamic world of network marketing.

- **Balancing Work and Personal Life**

Balancing work and personal life is a perennial challenge, and in the context of network marketing, where entrepreneurial endeavors often blend with personal responsibilities, finding equilibrium becomes paramount. Here's a guide on achieving a harmonious balance between your professional and personal life:

1. Establish Clear Boundaries:

   - Define clear boundaries between work and personal life. Set specific working hours and designate a dedicated workspace to create a distinction between professional and personal time and space.

2. Prioritize and Plan:

- Prioritize tasks and plan your day or week in advance. Identify crucial work commitments as well as personal priorities. A well-thought-out plan helps allocate time effectively.

3. Learn to Say No:

- Recognize your limitations and be willing to say no when necessary. Overcommitting can lead to stress and compromise the quality of both your work and personal life.

4. Time Blocking:

- Use time blocking techniques to allocate specific time slots for work, family, self-care, and other essential aspects of your life. This structured approach helps in maintaining balance and focus.

5. Quality Over Quantity:

- Emphasize the quality of your work over the quantity of time spent. Efficient, focused work allows you to accomplish more in less time, freeing up moments for personal pursuits.

6. Schedule Personal Time:

- Treat personal time with the same level of importance as work commitments. Schedule personal activities, family time, and self-care just as you would schedule work-related tasks.

7. Embrace Flexibility:

- Recognize that flexibility is a valuable aspect of network marketing. Embrace the ability to adjust your schedule based on your personal needs, but ensure that it doesn't compromise your overall balance.

8. Use Technology Wisely:

- Leverage technology to your advantage. Set boundaries on work-related notifications during personal time and vice versa. Smart use of technology can enhance productivity and help maintain balance.

9. Delegate and Outsource:

   - Delegate tasks when possible, both in your professional and personal life. Network marketing often involves building a team, and effective delegation is a skill that contributes to better work-life balance.

10. Regularly Reevaluate:

   - Regularly assess your work-life balance. As circumstances change, so do your priorities. Reevaluate and adjust your strategies to ensure continued harmony between your work and personal life.

11. Self-Care Matters:

   - Prioritize self-care as an integral part of your routine. Whether it's exercise, meditation, or simply downtime, taking care of yourself contributes to overall well-being and work-life balance.

12. Communicate Openly:

- Communicate openly with your team, family, and friends about your commitments and limitations. Clear communication fosters understanding and support, creating a positive environment.

13. Set Realistic Expectations:

- Be realistic about what you can accomplish in a given timeframe. Setting achievable goals helps in managing expectations and reducing stress associated with balancing work and personal life.

14. Celebrate Achievements:

- Celebrate both professional and personal achievements. Recognizing your successes, big or small, contributes to a positive mindset and reinforces the idea that balance is attainable.

Balancing work and personal life is an ongoing process that requires adaptability and conscious effort. By implementing these strategies, you can navigate the demands of network marketing while fostering a fulfilling personal life, creating a sustainable and harmonious balance.

- Dealing with Skepticism

Dealing with skepticism is an inherent challenge in network marketing, as individuals may approach your offerings with doubt or reservations. Navigating skepticism effectively is key to building trust and fostering successful relationships. Here's a guide on how to address skepticism in the context of network marketing:

1. Understand and Acknowledge:

- Recognize that skepticism is a natural response, especially in an industry where misconceptions exist. Understand that potential clients or team members may have reservations, and acknowledge their concerns.

2. Educate and Inform:
- Take a proactive approach by providing clear and accurate information about your products, services, or the network marketing opportunity. Education is a powerful tool for dispelling skepticism and building credibility.

3. Share Success Stories:
- Highlight success stories within your network marketing business. Real-life examples of individuals who have benefited from your products or have achieved success in the business can help overcome skepticism by showcasing tangible results.

4. Be Transparent:

- Foster trust by being transparent about the business model, compensation plan, and any potential risks. Transparency builds credibility and addresses concerns that may contribute to skepticism.

5. Address Specific Concerns:

- Listen actively to the specific concerns of skeptics and address them directly. Tailor your responses to their individual reservations, demonstrating a genuine understanding of their perspective.

6. Offer Trials or Samples:

- Provide opportunities for skeptics to experience your products or services firsthand. Offering trials, samples, or demonstrations allows individuals to assess the value directly, potentially alleviating skepticism.

7. Build Credibility Over Time:

- Consistently deliver on your promises and showcase the value of your offerings over time. Building credibility through sustained positive experiences is a powerful way to counter skepticism.

8. Establish Authority:

- Position yourself as an authority in your industry by staying informed about your products, industry trends, and relevant information. Authority contributes to trust and credibility, mitigating skepticism.

9. Encourage Questions:

- Create an open dialogue by encouraging individuals to ask questions. Addressing concerns openly and honestly fosters a sense of transparency and can ease skepticism.

10. Stay Calm and Professional:

- When faced with skepticism, maintain a calm and professional demeanor. Emotional reactions may exacerbate doubts, while a composed approach reinforces your confidence in what you offer.

11. Highlight Customer Testimonials:

- Showcase positive testimonials from satisfied customers. Testimonials serve as social proof, demonstrating that others have had positive experiences and diminishing skepticism.

12. Offer Guarantees:

- If applicable, provide guarantees or satisfaction assurances. Knowing that there is a safety net can alleviate skepticism and provide potential customers with confidence in their decision to try your products or services.

13. Showcase Your Values:

- Emphasize your commitment to ethical business practices, customer satisfaction, and integrity. Aligning your values with those of your potential customers can create a sense of trust and reduce skepticism.

14. Patience and Persistence:

- Overcoming skepticism may take time. Be patient and persistent in your efforts to build trust. Consistent, positive interactions can gradually shift skepticism into confidence.

Dealing with skepticism in network marketing is a process that involves proactive communication, transparency, and a commitment to building trust over time. By addressing concerns directly and showcasing the value of your offerings, you can gradually transform skepticism into a positive perception of your network marketing business.

Chapter 6:

Scaling Your Network Marketing Business

- Leadership and Team Building

Effective leadership and team building are fundamental pillars of success in network marketing. Building a cohesive and motivated team is essential for achieving common goals and fostering a positive working environment. Here's a guide on leadership and team building in the context of network marketing:

1. Lead by Example:

- Exemplify the qualities you expect from your team. Leading by example establishes credibility and sets the standard for professionalism, work ethic, and commitment.

2. Clear Vision and Goals:

- Clearly communicate the vision and goals of the network marketing team. A shared understanding of the overarching objectives aligns the team's efforts and fosters a sense of purpose.

3. Effective Communication:

- Establish open and transparent communication channels. Regularly update your team on important information, progress, and changes. Effective communication builds trust and cohesion.

4. Encourage Individual Strengths:

- Recognize and encourage the individual strengths of your team members. A diverse range of skills and talents contributes to a well-rounded and dynamic team.

5. Provide Training and Development:

- Invest in the training and development of your team members. Equip them with the knowledge and skills needed for success in network marketing. Ongoing education fosters confidence and competence.

6. Set Realistic Expectations:

- Set clear and realistic expectations for your team. Avoid creating undue pressure, and ensure that goals are achievable. Realistic expectations contribute to a positive team culture.

7. Promote a Positive Team Culture:

- Foster a positive team culture by promoting collaboration, mutual support, and a sense of camaraderie. A positive atmosphere enhances motivation and productivity.

8. Celebrate Achievements:

- Celebrate both individual and collective achievements. Recognition reinforces a sense of accomplishment and encourages continued effort and dedication.

9. Provide Constructive Feedback:

- Offer constructive feedback to help team members improve and grow. Constructive criticism, delivered with empathy, supports individual development and contributes to team success.

10. Delegate Effectively:

- Delegate tasks based on the strengths and capabilities of your team members. Effective delegation empowers individuals, promotes skill development, and contributes to overall team efficiency.

11. Encourage Innovation:

- Foster a culture of innovation where team members feel encouraged to share ideas and solutions. An innovative team adapts to challenges and stays ahead in the dynamic field of network marketing.

12. Crisis Management:

- Be prepared for challenges and crises. Effective leaders remain calm under pressure, assess situations objectively, and guide their teams through difficulties with resilience and determination.

13. Build Trust:

- Establish and nurture trust within your team. Trust is the foundation of a strong working relationship and enables effective collaboration and communication.

14. Accessibility and Approachability:

- Maintain an approachable demeanor and be accessible to your team. An open-door policy encourages team members to seek guidance and share concerns, fostering a supportive environment.

15. Team-Building Activities:

- Organize team-building activities that promote bonding and collaboration. These activities can be both fun and beneficial for strengthening the team's unity.

16. Adaptability:

- Demonstrate adaptability as a leader. In the ever-evolving landscape of network marketing, being able to adapt to changes and guide your team through transitions is crucial for success.

17. Encourage Healthy Competition:

- Foster a healthy sense of competition within the team. Encourage friendly competition that motivates individuals to strive for excellence while maintaining a supportive team environment.

By integrating these principles into your leadership approach, you can create a strong, motivated, and cohesive team in the field of network marketing. Effective leadership and team building contribute not only to individual success but also to the collective achievements of your network.

- Duplicating Success

"Duplicating success" is a key concept in network marketing, referring to the ability to replicate successful strategies and outcomes across your team. Creating a system that can be easily duplicated empowers team members to achieve similar success, contributing to the overall growth and prosperity of the network. Here's a guide on how to effectively duplicate success in network marketing:

1. Document Successful Strategies:

   - Begin by documenting the strategies, processes, and techniques that have led to success in your network marketing endeavors. This could include effective sales scripts, successful recruiting approaches, and proven marketing methods.

2. Create a Systematic Approach:

   - Develop a systematic approach that breaks down the success into manageable steps. A step-by-step system simplifies the process for team members, making it easier for them to follow and replicate.

3. Provide Comprehensive Training:

- Offer comprehensive training to your team. Ensure that each member understands the documented strategies and the reasoning behind them. A well-trained team is better equipped to duplicate success.

4. Focus on Fundamentals:

- Emphasize the fundamental principles that contribute to success. Whether it's consistent prospecting, effective communication, or strategic goal-setting, focusing on fundamentals ensures a strong foundation for duplicating success.

5. Encourage Consistency:

- Stress the importance of consistency in applying the proven strategies. Consistent effort over time is often the key to success in network marketing, and duplicating success relies on maintaining this consistency.

6. Highlight Success Stories:

- Share success stories within your network marketing team. Highlight individuals who have effectively duplicated success using the established strategies. Real-life examples provide inspiration and practical insights.

7. Implement Mentorship Programs:

- Establish mentorship programs within your team. Experienced members can guide and support newer team members in implementing successful strategies, accelerating the learning curve.

8. Regular Check-Ins and Support:

- Conduct regular check-ins to assess the progress of team members. Provide ongoing support, answer questions, and address challenges to ensure everyone feels supported in their efforts to duplicate success.

9. Adaptability:

- Recognize the need for adaptability within the system. Network marketing landscapes evolve, and what works today may need adjustments tomorrow. An adaptable system ensures ongoing relevance and effectiveness.

10. Simplify Processes:

- Keep processes as simple as possible. A complex system can be challenging to duplicate. Simplifying procedures makes it easier for team members, especially those new to network marketing, to replicate success.

11. Promote Team Collaboration:

- Encourage collaboration among team members. A collaborative environment facilitates the sharing of insights, tips, and experiences, creating a collective effort toward duplicating success.

12. Measure and Analyze Results:

- Implement mechanisms to measure and analyze results. Tracking progress allows you to identify what is working well and where adjustments may be needed to enhance the success-duplication process.

13. Celebrate Milestones:

- Celebrate milestones and achievements within the team. Recognizing and acknowledging accomplishments fosters motivation and reinforces the idea that duplicating success is both attainable and rewarding.

14. Provide Tools and Resources:

- Equip your team with the necessary tools and resources to implement successful strategies. This could include marketing materials, training videos, or software that streamlines certain processes.

15. Lead by Example:

- Lead by example in duplicating success. Demonstrate the effectiveness of the system by applying it to your own efforts. Your success becomes a powerful testament to the viability of the strategies you've implemented.

By focusing on creating a duplicable system and providing the necessary support and resources, you empower your network marketing team to replicate success. Duplicating success is not only about achieving individual goals but also about fostering a culture of shared success within your entire network.

- Long-Term Sustainability and Growth

Long-term sustainability and growth are paramount in the world of network marketing. Building a resilient and expanding network requires strategic planning, adaptability, and a focus on sustainable practices. Here's a comprehensive guide on achieving long-term sustainability and growth in network marketing:

1. Establish a Strong Foundation:

- Lay the groundwork for long-term success by building a strong foundation. This includes clear business goals, a well-defined target audience, and a robust understanding of your products or services.

2. Focus on Product Quality:

- Sustain growth by offering high-quality products or services. Customer satisfaction is central to long-term success, and quality offerings build a positive reputation within your network.

3. Build Relationships, Not Just Sales:

- Prioritize relationship-building over transactional interactions. Developing genuine connections with your team and customers fosters loyalty, trust, and a sustainable network.

4. Implement Effective Training Programs:

- Invest in ongoing training programs for your team. Equipping them with the necessary skills and knowledge ensures continuous improvement and contributes to the longevity of your network.

5. Diversify Revenue Streams:

- Foster long-term sustainability by diversifying your revenue streams. Explore complementary products or services that align with your existing offerings, providing additional value to your network.

6. Stay Informed About Industry Trends:

- Keep abreast of industry trends and changes. Adapting to emerging trends ensures that your network marketing strategies remain relevant, positioning you for sustained growth.

7. Encourage a Culture of Learning:

- Foster a culture of continuous learning within your team. An environment that encourages education and skill development contributes to adaptability and long-term success.

8. Embrace Technology:

- Leverage technology to streamline processes and enhance communication. Staying current with technological advancements can give your network a competitive edge and support sustainable growth.

9. Implement Scalable Systems:

- Design systems and processes that are scalable. As your network grows, scalable systems accommodate increased demands efficiently, ensuring smooth operations and sustained growth.

10. Prioritize Customer Retention:

- Place a strong emphasis on customer retention. Building lasting relationships with customers encourages repeat business and word-of-mouth referrals, contributing to long-term sustainability.

11. Strategic Marketing and Branding:

- Develop a strategic marketing and branding strategy. Consistent and well-executed branding reinforces your network's identity, making it more memorable and attractive to potential customers and team members.

12. Adaptability and Flexibility:

- Cultivate adaptability and flexibility within your network. The ability to pivot and adjust strategies in response to changing market conditions ensures resilience and sustained growth over time.

13. Encourage Leadership Development:

- Foster leadership development within your team. Identifying and nurturing leaders contributes to the overall strength of your network and creates a sustainable framework for growth.

14. Set Realistic Goals:

- Establish realistic and achievable long-term goals. A clear vision and well-defined objectives provide direction, motivating your team and creating a roadmap for sustained growth.

15. Measure and Analyze Performance:

- Implement performance metrics and regularly analyze results. Tracking key performance indicators (KPIs) helps identify areas for improvement and informs strategic decisions for long-term sustainability.

16. Cultivate a Positive Team Culture:

- Foster a positive team culture based on trust, collaboration, and mutual support. A cohesive team is more resilient and better positioned for sustained growth.

17. Compliance and Ethical Practices:

- Prioritize compliance with industry regulations and ethical business practices. Upholding high standards contributes to a positive reputation and long-term trust from customers and team members.

By integrating these principles into your network marketing approach, you can create a foundation for long-term sustainability and growth. A holistic and strategic approach, coupled with a commitment to continuous improvement, positions your network for success over the long term.

www.ingramcontent.com/pod-product-compliance
Lightning Source LLC
Chambersburg PA
CBHW062347290526
45794CB00005B/2132